FOSTER & ALLEN
···
SONGBOOK

Wise Publications
London / New York / Sydney

Exclusive Distributors:

Music Sales Limited
8/9 Frith Street, London W1V 5TZ, England.

Music Sales Pty Limited
120 Rothschild Avenue, Rosebery, NSW 2018, Australia.

This book © Copyright 1991 by Wise Publications
Order No.AM86298
ISBN 0.7119.2773.1

Compiled by Pat Conway
Music processed by Seton Music Graphics

Music Sales' complete catalogue lists thousands of titles
and is free from your local music shop, or direct from Music Sales Limited.
Please send a cheque/postal order for £1.50 for postage to:
Music Sales Limited, Newmarket Road, Bury St. Edmunds, Suffolk IP33 3YB.

Your Guarantee of Quality:

As publishers, we strive to produce every book to the highest commercial standards.

All the music has been freshly engraved, and the book has been carefully designed to
minimise awkward page turns and to make playing from it a real pleasure.

Particular care has been given to specifying acid-free, neutral-sized paper which
has not been chlorine bleached but produced with special regard for the environment.
Throughout, the printing and binding have been planned to ensure a sturdy,
attractive publication which should give years of enjoyment.

If your copy fails to meet our high standards, please inform us and we will gladly replace it.

Printed in the United Kingdom by
Caligraving Limited, Thetford, Norfolk.

Maggie

Traditional. Arranged by Foster & Allen

creak - ing old mill _____ is still, Mag - gie, ___ Since ___ you and ___ I were ___ young.

1. & 2. young. _____ They young. _____ **3.**

2. They say that I'm feeble with age, Maggie
My steps are much slower than then.
My face is a well-written page, Maggie
And time all alone was the pen.

They say we have outlived our time, Maggie
As dated as songs that we've sung.
But to me you're as fair as you were, Maggie
When you and I were young.

(Repeat last four lines)

Old Flames

Words & Music by Pebe Siebert & Hugh Moffat

eye of for-got-ten de - sire,_____ With a word or a touch, Lord

I could have re - kin - dled that fire._____ But

old flames can't hold a can - dle to you,_____

No one_____ can light up my life like you do._____

2. Sometimes at night I think of the lovers I've known
And I remember how holding them
Helped me not feel so alone.
Then I feel you beside me and even their memories are gone,
Like stars in the night, lost in the sweet light of dawn.

Repeat Chorus twice:—

9

After All These Years

Words & Music by Coleman & Kennedy

My dar - ling come to me Sit you down ea - si - ly

and rest a - while Near the soft fire light, cold as the

night. But warm is my heart with pride hav - ing you by my side

You're still my guid - ing light af - ter a - ll these years.

Your soft as - sur - ing ways the rock I lean on

Saw me through my dark - est days when all hope had

gone. You're still the on - ly one

2. Time from me passes on and I'm growing old
   A lifetime nearly gone I cannot unfold
   Nights dark and cold.
   But warm is your hand in mine
   Feeble with ageless time
   The light of love still shines
   After all these years.

Molly Darling

Traditional. Arranged by Foster & Allen

thine. _____ Mol - ly ___ sweet - est, ___ fair - est, ___ dear - est, ___ Look up dar - ling tell me this, ____ ___ Do you love me ___ Mol - ly ___ dar - ling, Let your ans - wer be a kiss. _____

I Will Love You All My Life

Words & Music by C. A. Landsborough

o - ther cheek,_____ But I will love you all my life.
love you so,_____

I can ne - ver do things right by you,_____ I'm the kind of man who
E - ven though you ne - ver care for me,_____

mud - dles through,_____ You can find mis - takes in all I do,_____
Dar - ling how I wish that you could see,_____

____ But I will love you all my life. Some - thing foo - lish hap - pens
____ That I will love you all my life.

and you see_____ In the mid-dle of it all there's me,_____

Seems I cause you so much mi-se-ry_____ But I will love you all my

Chorus

life._____ All my

life, all I own, Ev-ery-

We Will Make Love

Words & Music by Ronald Hulme

love so true is on - ly for you So re - mem - ber you're

mine, you're mine all the time, When the sun takes the

place of the moon in the sky. We'll go on a jour - ney

you____ and I_____ To a far dis - tant

2. I wish we could wed but we are too young,
But one day I know wedding bells will be rung
For you and for me, we'll promise to be
So faithful and true, I love you.
Oh yes I love you.

Chorus:—

3. Now it's getting late and we must part,
But before I go I'll leave you my heart.
So don't shed a tear I'll always be near,
I'll hold you so tight and kiss you goodnight.
Oh yes I'll kiss you goodnight.

Chorus:—

A Bunch Of Thyme

Traditional. Arranged by Foster & Allen

2. For thyme it is a precious thing
And thyme brings all things to my mind.
Thyme, with all its labours
Along with all its joys,
Thyme brings all things to my mind.

3. Once she had a bunch of thyme,
She thought it never would decay,
Then came a lusty sailor
Who chanced to pass her way.
He stole her bunch of thyme away.

4. The sailor gave to her a rose,
A rose that never would decay,
He gave it to her
To keep her reminded
Of when he stole her thyme away.

5. *Repeat Chorus*

6. For thyme it is a precious thing
And thyme brings all things to my mind.
Thyme, with all its labours
Along with all its joys,
Thyme brings all things to an end.

Come Back Paddy Reilly To Bally James Duff

Traditional. Arranged by Foster & Allen

2. My mother once told me the day I was born
The day that I first saw the light
I looked down the street on that very first morn
And gave a great crow of delight
Now most new-born babies appear in a huff
And start with a sorrowful squall
But I knew I was born in Ballyjamesduff
And that's why I smiled on them all.
That baby's a man now
He's toil-worn and tough
Still whispers come over the sea
Come back Paddy Reilly to Ballyjamesduff
Come home Paddy Reilly to me.

Red River Valley

Traditional. Arranged by Foster & Allen

1. From this val - ley they say you are go - ing, I will miss your bright eyes and sweet smile For you're

2. Won't you think of the valley you're leaving
Oh how lonely, how sad I will be.
Oh please think of the fond heart you're breaking
And the grief you are causing to me.

Chorus:—

Blue Eyes Crying In The Rain

Words & Music by Fred Rose

In the twi - light glow I ___ see you. ___

Blue eyes cry - ing ___ in the rain. ___

When we kissed good-bye and par - ted _____ I

knew we'd ne - ver ___ meet a - gain.

Love is like ___ a dy - ing em - ber. _____

On - ly me - mo - ries ___ re - main.

Through the a - ges___ I'll re - mem - ber___

Blue eyes cry - ing___ in the rain. ___ rain.___

___ Blue eyes cry - ing___ in the rain.___

2. Now my hair has turned to silver
   All my life I've loved in vain
   I can see your star in heaven
   Blue eyes crying in the rain.
   Some day when we meet up yonder
   We'll stroll hand in hand again
   In a land that knows no parting
   Blue eyes crying in the rain.

Silver Threads Among The Gold

Traditional. Arranged by Foster & Allen

1.Dar - ling I am grow - ing old,___ Sil - ver threads a - mong the gold Shine up -

on my brow to - day,_____

Life is fad - ing___ fast a - way.

But my dar - ling___ you will

be, will be al - ways

2. When your hair is silver white
   And your cheeks no longer bright
   With the roses of the May
   I will kiss your lips and say
   Oh my darling mine alone, alone
   You have never older grown.
   Yes my darling mine alone
   You have never older grown.

3. Love can never more grow old,
   Locks may lose their brown and gold,
   Cheeks may fade and hollow grow
   But the hearts that love will know
   Never never winter's frost and chill
   Summer warmth is in them still.
   Never winter's frost and chill
   Summer's warmth is in them still.

Just For Old Times Sake

Words & Music by Sid Tepper & Roy C. Bennett

then. I know now I know _____ the

day I ___ let you go I made my great-est___ mis-take.

If you loved me then you can love me once a-

gain. Won't you try just for old time's sake.

I Still Love You

Traditional. Arranged by Foster & Allen

I still love you___ as I

did in___ yes - ter - day, Ma - ny years have gone

by tho' it seems just like a day. It's no

won - der___ that I___ love you,___ you have been so kind and

true, There will ne - ver___ be a - no - ther,___ it will

al - ways be just___ you. We've come a long way to -

ge - ther___ and you've proved your love is___ true. My

The Old Rustic Bridge By The Mill

Words & Music by Campbell & Cassidy

1. I'm think - ing to -

night_____ of the old_____ rus - tic bridge_____

that bends o'er the mur - mur - ing

stream._____ It was there

Mag - gie dear with our hearts full of___

cheer, we strayed 'neath the moon's___

gen - tle beam._____ 'Twas
there   I   first met you,_____ the
light_____ in your eyes_____ a - woke
in   my   heart   a   sweet____ prayer._____

neath it a stream_____ gen - tly

rip - pled,_____ a -

round it the birds loved to trill._____

Though now far a - way

still my thoughts fond - ly stray_____ to the
old rus - tic bridge_____ by the mill._____

2.   I keep in my memory our love of the past,
   With me it's as bright as of old,
   For deep in my heart it was planted to last,
   In absence it never grows cold.
   I think of you, darling, when lonely at night
   And when all is peaceful and still,
   My heart wanders back in a dream of delight
   To the old rustic bridge by the mill.

Chorus:—